A
Comforting Truth
To Know Him Is to Be Like Him

Stanley J. Martin Payne

TEACH Services, Inc.
P U B L I S H I N G
www.TEACHServices.com • (800) 367-1844

Copyright © 2017 Stanley J. Martin Payne

Copyright © 2017 TEACH Services, Inc.

ISBN-13: 978-1-4796-0806-5 (Paperback)

ISBN-13: 978-1-4796-0807-2 (ePub)

ISBN-13: 978-1-4796-0808-9 (Mobi)

Library of Congress Control Number: 2017910247

TEACH Services, Inc.

P U B L I S H I N G

www.TEACHServices.com ● (800) 367-1844

Table of Contents

Introduction

In John 17, the Bible records the high priestly prayer of Jesus with His disciples prior to being betrayed and led away to be crucified. The fact that Jesus prayed was not unusual, for He was a Man of prayer. He was not just a Man of prayer, but He prayed with the assurance that the Father would always hear Him. "Father, I thank You that You have heard Me. And I know You always hear Me, but because of the people who are standing by I said this, that they may believe that You sent Me" (John 11:41–42).

This time was different; this prayer was different. First, we consider the scope and breadth of this prayer. He prayed not just for His twelve current disciples, but for all those who would believe in Him through their message. Yes, He prayed for you and me. Acknowledging that he prayed for us, perhaps we may ask ourselves the question: 'Has His prayer for us been answered?'

Second, we consider the timing of this intercessory prayer. Here Jesus recognizes and proclaims that this phase of His work had come to an end. He states in John 17:4, "I have glorified You on the earth. I have finished the work which You have given Me to do." Then He fully acknowledges His oneness with the Father, for He said in verse 5 of the same chapter, "And now, O Father glorify Me together with Yourself with the glory which I had with You before the world was." He later continued, "that they all may be one, as You, Father, are in Me and I in You; that they also maybe one in Us, that the world may believe that You sent Me" (vs. 21).

Third, Jesus knew that immediately before Him was Gethsemane, the cross, and the cruel crucifixion. We would think that this should've been foremost on His mind; instead He seemed to be focused on the eternal life of His current disciples and the rest of His followers through the ages to the end of time. "I do not pray for these alone, but also for those who will believe in Me through their word" (v. 20).

How could He, at such a moment in time, be so selfless? How could He look passed and beyond His imminent suffering and focus on our eternal destiny with such laser-like precision? Oh, What love! The joy of seeing sinners saved into His eternal kingdom was always before Him and would eclipse the weight of His own suffering. Thus, even at this trying hour, He, "who for the joy that was set before Him endured the cross, despising the shame" (Heb.12:2), had you and me on His mind.

Chapter 1

Jesus Prayed for You

"And this is the will of Him who sent Me, that everyone who sees the Son and believes in Him may have everlasting life" (John 6:40)

As we consider this most remarkable intercessory prayer, we will recognize that Jesus focused primarily on the eternal destiny of the twelve and those in every succeeding generation who would believe on Him because of their message.

In John 17:3, Jesus implicitly expressed the desire to have His disciples and all who would subsequently believe in Him get to know Him and the Father. "And this is eternal life, that they may know You, the only true God, and Jesus Christ whom You have sent." Then, very explicitly, He asked the Father for the sanctification of His followers and their oneness with Him and the Father. "Sanctify them by Your truth. Your word is truth….That they all may be one, as You, Father, are in Me and I in You; that they also may be one in Us, that the world may believe that You sent me" (John 17:17, 21).

As we consider these three aspects of this remarkable intercessory prayer, perhaps we may be find that the process by which these (knowing Him, sanctification, and becoming one with Him as He is with the Father) are accomplished is very much the same, indeed, in quite the same manner. We can readily acknowledge that knowing Him, sanctification, and becoming one with Him are not the work of a moment, but rather the work of a lifetime. In Proverbs 4:18 we are reminded that: "the path of the just is like the shining sun, That shines ever brighter unto the perfect day."

What does knowing God and Jesus Christ whom He sent actually do for you? According to Jesus, your eternal life is dependent on it. Then what is it? What is knowing God? **Knowing God is the lifelong process of becoming more and more like Jesus as a consequence of a consistent relationship with Him.**

Chapter 2

He Wants You to Know Him

"And this is life eternal, that they may know You"
(John 17:3).

"Father, the hour has come. Glorify Your Son, that Your Son also may glorify You, as You have given Him authority over all flesh, that He should give eternal life to as many as You have given Him. And this is eternal life, that they may know You, the only true God, and Jesus Christ whom You have sent" (John 17:1–3).

In this passage, Jesus seems to suggest that eternal life; and knowing God the Father and Him are inseparable. Simply put, we cannot have eternal life without knowing God the Father and Jesus the Son.

As we proceed, there are a couple things from this passage which we may want to consider.

The first thing is determining the difference between knowing God the Father and knowing Jesus. Is there even a difference?

In John 14:1–11, Jesus makes it very clear that to know Him is to know the Father. In fact, He reveals the Father; therefore, if you have seen Him, you have seen the Father. Jesus further points out that our access to the Father is only through Him; for he's not only the truth and the life, but also the way.

"If you had known Me, you would have known My Father also; and from now on you know Him and have seen Him." Phillip said to Him "Lord, show us The Father, and it is sufficient for us," Jesus said to him, "have I been with you so long and yet you have not known Me, Philip? He who has seen Me has seen the Father; so how can you say show us the Father? Do you not believe that I am in the Father and the Father in Me? The words I speak to you I do not speak on My own authority; but the Father who dwells in Me does the works. Believe Me that I am in the Father and the Father in Me..." (John 14:7–11).

This same truth is brought out in the prayer of Jesus for the unity of His followers. The disciples were men of very different backgrounds, habits, and natural characteristics. In order for them to effectively do the work of being Christ's messengers to the world, they needed to be able speak with one voice, having the same thoughts, motives, and purpose. This unity could only be achieved as they became one with Jesus like He was one with The Father. Simply put, they all had to become like Jesus. "I do not pray for these alone, but also for those who will believe in Me through their word; that they all maybe one, as You, Father, are in Me and I in You; that they also maybe one in Us that the world may believe that You sent Me" (John 17:20–21).

"God who at various times and in various ways spoke in time past to the fathers by the prophets, has in these last days spoken to us by His Son, whom He has appointed heir of all things, through whom also He made the worlds; who being the brightness of His glory and the express image of His person, and upholding all things by the word of His power..." (Heb. 1:1–3).

Second, we can conclude from the above that to know Jesus is to know God the Father. Therefore, knowing God and Jesus Christ whom He sent would be the result of the same process. Therefore, for the purpose of this exercise we want to take a close look at the lifelong process of becoming more and more like Jesus as a consequence of getting to know Him through a close and consistent relationship with Him.

In a very general sense, we say we know someone after we have acquired some information or facts about them. This knowledge is usually the result of a number of singular events, which allow us to obtain and accumulate information about that person. Thus, we say we know our friends, family, coworkers, and so on. Usually we know those of our household, those with whom we spend more time, in a much more intimate way.

The Scriptures reveal the oneness which Jesus had with the Father from eternity past through eternity future as the second person of the Godhead. The Scriptures also reveal a very close, personal, consistent, and dynamic relationship between the Father and the Son, as demonstrated in the life of Jesus as He lived on this earth.

A relationship which manifested itself in the language of humanity, in human terms and acts so we could more readily understand and identify with it. In a larger sense, His life lived as the Son of man, totally dependent on the Father, shows us how humanity, in cooperation with divinity, can overcome all the snares of the enemy. This is His goal for us, that we enter a relationship with Him in which we are fully submissive to and totally dependent on Him as He was on the Father.

"Behold," John writes, "what manner of love the Father has bestowed on us, that we should be called the children of God!... Beloved, now are we children of God; and it has not yet been revealed what we shall be, but we know that when He is revealed, we shall be like Him, for we shall see Him as He is" (1 John 3:1–2).

With that said, what is Jesus asking here of His followers? Is it for us to gather as much statistics on His life as we can? Is it for us to accumulate and even document every detail of His life we can find?

The word "know," as used in John 17:3, is the Greek word Ginosko (Ghin-oce-ko), which theologians agree is similar to the word used in the Septuagint (Greek Old Testament) of Genesis to describe the intimate relationship between Adam and Eve (see Gen. 4:1). In Jewish tradition, this word is sometimes used in the idiomatic form in reference to the relationship between a man and a woman, a husband and a wife. Jesus is therefore talking about a personal relationship with Him, one that is close and consistent; one that enables us to have an experimental knowledge of Him. This experience allows us to see Him as He is— full of love and compassion. That love begets love and so the desire to be like Him is awakened in us, and through the Holy Spirit we become more and more like Him, transformed into His image. With time and consistency, we get to know Him better, our view of Him becomes clearer, and our nothingness becomes more evident. We see in Him one who loves us, then our desire to be like Him gets stronger and stronger. God responds to our desire by changing our character to be like that of our Savior through the transforming power of His Holy Spirit.

We get to know those in our own household better than we do others. The reason is we spend more time with them. Perhaps more accurately, we spend more quality time with them. It will be the same for our relationship with Jesus. As we spend more quality time with our Master the more we become like Him.

An inspired writer for our time puts it this way in commenting on the transforming experience of the Apostle John:

"The depth and fervor of John's affection for his Master was not the cause of Christ's love for him, but the effect of that love. John desired to become like Jesus, and under the transforming influence of the love of Christ he did become meek and lowly. Self was hidden in Jesus. Above all his companions, John yielded himself to the power of that wondrous life. He says, 'The life was manifested, and we have seen it.' 'And of His fullness have all we received, and grace for grace.' 1 John 1:2; John 1:16. **John knew the Savior by an experimental knowledge.** His Master's lessons were *graven* on his soul. When he testified of the Savior's grace, his simple language was eloquent with the love that pervaded his whole being.—AA 544.2

"It was John's deep love for Christ which led him always to desire to be close by His side. The Savior loved all the Twelve, but John's was the most receptive spirit. He was younger than the others, and with more of the child's confiding trust he opened his heart to Jesus. Thus, he came more into sympathy with Christ, and through him the Savior's deepest spiritual teaching was communicated to the people.

"Jesus loves those who represent the Father, and John could talk of the Father's love as no other of the disciples could. He revealed to his fellow men that which he felt in his own soul, representing in his character the attributes of God. The glory of the Lord was expressed in his face. The beauty of holiness which had transformed him shone with a Christ like radiance from his countenance. **In adoration and love he beheld the Savior until likeness to Christ and fellowship with Him became his one desire, and in his character, was reflected the character of his Master."**—AA 545.1–2

Of the Apostle Paul, she wrote, "The apostle Paul had all the privileges of a Roman citizen. He was not behind in the Hebrew education, for he had learned at the feet of Gamaliel; but all this did not enable him to reach the highest standard. With all this scientific and literary education, he was, until Christ was revealed to him, in as complete darkness as are many at this time. **Paul became fully conscious that to know Jesus Christ by an experimental knowledge was for his present and eternal good. He saw the necessity of reaching a high standard."**—6BC 1084.6

The more quality time we spend with Jesus, the better we get to know Him. The more time we spend with Jesus, the more we understand how loving He is, how much He cares for us, and the more appreciative we become of the sacrifice He made for us on Calvary. The most amazing thing about such a relationship is that the more we see of Him, the more we get to know Him, and the more we become like Him, for by beholding Him we become changed. "But we all, with unveiled face, beholding as in a mirror the glory of the Lord, are being transformed into the same image from glory to glory, just as by the Spirit of The Lord" (2 Cor. 3:18).

This is the great theme of the Bible; this is the story of redemption—how God, through the life, death, resurrection, and intercessory work of Jesus, would restore His image in fallen humanity. Therefore, like Adam, when he came from the Creator's hand, we can again be like Him. This is the preparation needed for eternal life. No wonder the burden of His heart, as expressed in John 17:3, was for His people to know Him. As we get to know the only true God and Jesus Christ whom He sent, we will share the testimony of

John: "Behold what manner of love the Father has bestowed on us, that we should be called the children of God" (1 John 3:1)! Get to know Him and you will understand that He loves you with an everlasting love. Get to know Him and you will have the assurance that nothing shall separate you from His love. Get to know Him moment by moment, day by day, through the experience of a consistent relationship, and you will learn to love as He loved, for by beholding you will become changed. You will become more and more like Him.

Chapter 3

God Loves You

"Behold what manner of love the Father has bestowed on us, that we should be called the children of God"
(1 John 3:1)!

Our world is such an evil place, perhaps it is difficult to imagine that it was not always like this. Yes, there actually was a time when the human family was just like God, its Maker. When Adam came from the Creator's hand, he had a big heart of love, just like his Maker does—a heart that knew no jealousy, hate, pride, fear, anger, greed, guilt, or any of the strange emotions that we all experience today. Man was made in the image of God (see Gen. 1:26).

Jesus died for, and to take away, our jealousy, hate, pride, fear, anger, greed, guilt, and all of the strange emotions we may experience. He longs to restore that broken relationship with the human family. He wants to restore His image in each of us, but He knows it is not the work of an instant, but rather the work of a lifetime. Therefore, he pleads, "Come now, and let us reason together…though your sins are like scarlet, they shall be as white as snow; though they be red like crimson, they shall be as wool" (Isa. 1:18).

Jesus prayed that you would get to know Him, so you could become like Him. Is that prayer being answered in your life?

One of the truly amazing things about the prayer of Jesus recorded in John 17 is found in verse 23: "I in them, and You in Me; that they may be made perfect in one, and that the world may know that You have sent Me, **and have loved them as You have loved Me**." Can you imagine that God loves you like He loves His wonderful, loving, sinless Son? Think about that for a moment; yes, love far beyond human comprehension. We could only exclaim, like John did, "Behold what manner of love the Father has bestowed on us, that we should be called children of God!" God loves us and has promised that nothing can separate us from that love. "For I am persuaded that neither death nor life, nor angels nor principalities nor powers, nor things present nor things to come, nor height nor depth, nor any other created thing, shall separate us from the love of God which is in Christ Jesus our Lord" (Rom. 8:38–39).

Yes, friends, God longs to answer the prayer of Jesus in the life of each one of us. Are you ready to enter a forever relationship with Jesus so that day by day, moment by moment, you get to know Him and consequently become more and more like Him?

Chapter 4

Jesus is Still the Answer

How far have we come?
How close are we to having come "full circle?"

It is difficult to imagine a world without pain, stress, sorrow, death, hate, sickness, and cruelty. However, there was a time when the human family knew only peace, joy, and contentment. The earth was still in its infancy; Adam and Eve, as they came from the Creator's hand, were like God, created in His image. God looked at everything He made, including the first man and woman, and declared that it was very good.

Today, long removed from the home of our fore parents, we have sickness, suffering, pain, and death. Disasters, natural and man-made, all seem so normal.

Many believe not only that it has always been this way, but more importantly, that it will always be this way.

We live in a time of tremendous medical advancement. Today's medical technology leaves us in amazement, from super powerful drugs to astoundingly invasive and revealing medical equipment. Sadly, we must acknowledge that with all the aforementioned medical advancements, we still suffer and die. The earth, now approximately 6,000 years old, is all too frequently the scene of tragedy and heartbreak. The prevailing lawlessness with its cruelty, the toll of natural and man-made disasters leave behind the reality of suffering, pain, and sorrow, sometimes beyond that which human language can describe.

We should, however, not be discouraged, for Jesus has promised to make things better. Therefore, with good reason and for our benefit, He offered such an impassioned prayer, asking the Father to make us one in Him and so live in preparation for the time when there will be no more sickness, tears, pain, or death.

As Jesus lifted up his eyes to heaven during this remarkable intercessory prayer, He, whose prophetic eye took in all the events of every age, must have seen before Him Gethsemane and the soldiers coming to take Him like a regular prisoner. He knew the humiliation and insults He would endure at the hands of Annas and Caiaphas the high priests, the mockery displayed in the court of Pilate, the cries of those who called for Barabbas to go free, and the mob calling "crucify him, crucify him". Yet he had heaven on His mind. He had you and your eternal destiny on His mind.

Cavalry loomed large before Him, but it could not distract Him from His mission of revealing the true nature of the God of heaven—a God who "so loved the world that he gave His only begotten Son, that whoever believes in Him should not perish but have everlasting life" (John 3:16). He proclaimed, "I have glorified You on the earth, I have finished the work which You have given Me to do. And now O Father glorify Me together with Yourself with glory which I had with You before the world began" (John 17:4, 5).

The Apostle Paul captures this theme beautifully. Paul had become like his Master as a consequence of a consistent relationship with Him. Ever since that encounter with Jesus on his way to Damascus, Paul, who was so moved by the amazing love of Jesus as demonstrated at Calvary, could only exclaim, "For I determine not to know anything among you except Jesus Christ and Him crucified" (1 Cor. 2:2). For Paul and all humanity, that cross, like a great "stature of liberty," shines from a little hill called Calvary, beckoning every lost sinner to come home.

He who had boldly declared that he wanted to know nothing but Jesus and Him crucified, was now ready to follow in his Master's footsteps. "I have fought the good fight, I have finished the race, I have kept the faith. Finally, there is laid up for me the crown of righteousness, which the Lord, the righteous Judge, will give to me on that Day, and not to me only but also to all who have loved His appearing." (2 Tim. 4:7–8).

The prayer of Jesus had been answered in the life of this faithful apostle. Paul had gotten to know Jesus, became "sanctified by the truth", and became like His Master; for to know Him is to be like Him. To be sanctified by the truth is to become like Him. This is a most comforting truth.

Paul states in 2 Timothy 1:12, "for this reason I also suffer these things; nevertheless, I am not ashamed, for I know whom I have believed and am persuaded that He is able to keep what I have committed to Him until that day."

This same assurance can be yours if, moment by moment, day by day, the prayer of Jesus is being answered in your life. Are you getting to know him? Are you being sanctified by the truth? Are you becoming like Him?

Chapter 5

Be Like Him—
It's Not Optional

*"But we know that when He is revealed,
we shall be like Him" (1 John 3:2).*

To be like Jesus is not optional. If we would live with Jesus eternally, we must become like Him here; yes, we must know Him by that experimental knowledge, the result of a consistent relationship with Him. This comforting truth lies at the core of our salvation. No one is fit to enter heaven or inherit eternal life for which Jesus prayed without this needed preparation. We are all invited to that great feast represented in the Bible as a wedding feast. If we would have permanent entry, the garment must be appropriate. Having been clothed in His righteousness, we would have gotten to know Him by the experience of a consistent relationship. We would have become like Him. His character would have been reproduced in us like it had been in Enoch. Enoch "walked" with God, the Scriptures tell us, for three hundred years. What a relationship! What a walk! Are you walking with Jesus?

Jesus is ready for some quality time with you. Are you having enough or any quality time with Him? "Behold, I stand at the door and knock", says Jesus. "If anyone hears My voice and opens the door, I will come in to him and dine with him, and he with Me" (Rev. 3:20). He is talking about a long-term relationship, one which is close, personal, and consistent. He wants to have that "covenant" relationship with you and all of us.

"But as many as received Him, to them gave He power to become the sons of God, even to them that believe on His name" (John 1:12). Will You Open the Door? Jesus says, "'Behold, I stand at the door, and knock.' Will we let Him in? He would not have us stand at this time, amid the perils of the last days, in our own finite strength.... It is our privilege to walk in the sunshine of His presence, and to weave into the characters we are forming the golden threads of cheerfulness, gratitude, forbearance, and love. We may thus show the power of divine grace, and reflect light from Heaven amid all the frets and irritations that come to us day by day.... Then why do we go stumbling along without light?"—OHC 352.2

"How precious is the promise, 'I will come in to him, and will sup with him, and he with Me.' Oh, the love, the wondrous love of God! After all our Luke warmness and sins, He says, Return unto Me, and I will return unto thee, and will heal all thy backslidings."—OHC 352.5

This is the great theme of the Bible—from Genesis to Revelation—how the God of heaven would leave nothing undone in order that the broken relationship between Him and sinful humanity might be restored; that humanity would again bear His image. He is knocking at the door of your heart. He patiently awaits your response. Will you let Him into your heart? He wants to restore that which Adam lost. For "God was in Christ reconciling the world to Himself" (2 Cor. 5:19).

Chapter 6

Meet Him and Be Better For It

No one encounters Jesus and is the same there after.

Accept Him and better for it, reject Him and be worst off for having met Him.

"Beholding Christ means studying His life as given in His Word. We are to dig for truth as for hidden treasure. We are to fix our eyes upon Christ. When we take Him as our personal Savior, this gives us boldness to approach the throne of grace. By beholding, we become changed—morally assimilated to the One who is perfect in character. By receiving His imputed righteousness, through the transforming power of the Holy Spirit, we become like Him. The image of

Christ is cherished, and it captivates the whole being. —12MR 55.3

"God takes men as they are, and educates them for His service, if they will yield themselves to Him. The Spirit of God, received into the soul, quickens all its faculties. Under the guidance of the Holy Spirit, the mind that is devoted unreservedly to God, develops harmoniously, and is strengthened to comprehend and fulfill the requirements of God. The weak, vacillating character becomes changed to one of strength and steadfastness. Continual devotion establishes so close a relation between Jesus and His disciples that the Christian becomes like his Master in character. He has clearer, broader views. His discernment is more penetrative, his judgment better balance. So quickened is he by the life-giving power of the Sun of Righteousness that he is enabled to bear much fruit to the glory of God." —SD 33.5

"The Spirit re-creates, refines, and sanctifies human beings, fitting them to become members of the royal family, children of the heavenly King." —RC 133.3

As we are changed into His likeness, and in word and deed act like He would, the world takes notice that we have been with Jesus and learned of Him, as it did of the apostles in the early church.

"Now when they saw the boldness of Peter and John, and perceived that they were uneducated and untrained men, they marveled. And they realized that they had been with Jesus" (Acts 4:13).

Chapter 7
Jesus Reveals His Character

"In the volume of the book it is written of Me"
(Ps. 40:7)

How can we get to know Him? Where can we best behold Him? Where has He been most thoroughly revealed? Where has He revealed Himself in the language of humanity so we can become acquainted with Him? "Then said I, Lo I come: In the volume of the book it is written of Me" (Ps. 40:7, KJV).

Like a wonderful love letter to every child of humanity, in His Word God has revealed Himself. In the Bible, He is revealed as The God of love, "full of compassion, and gracious, longsuffering, and plenteous in mercy and truth" (Ps. 86:15).

We see Him as the One who so loved that He gave all. We see Him as the only One who would lay down His life for His friends. "Greater love hath no man than this, that a man lay down His life for His friends" (John 15:13).

In the volume of the book we see Him as the all-powerful God who stepped out into nothing, "spoke, and it was done; He commanded, and it stood fast." (Ps. 33:9).

In the volume of the book we hear Him say, "peace, be still," to the raging wind and the roaring sea, and they obeyed His will; those who witnessed could only exclaim, "who can this be, that even the winds and sea obey Him!" (Mark 4:39, 41). He gave sight to the blind, hearing to the deaf, and firm steps to the crippled. In the volume of the book we hear Him speak with such authority that His hearers could only stand in astonishment. He gave bread to the hungry, hope to the hopeless, and yes, life to the dead.

In the volume of the book, He is the "Lily of the valley, the bright and morning star, the One altogether lovely. He is Wonderful, Counselor, Mighty God, the Everlasting Father, Prince of Peace." Yet He was a Man of sorrows, for "He was wounded for our transgressions, He was bruised for our iniquities: the chastisement for our peace was upon Him, and by His stripes we are healed" (Isa. 9:6; Isa. 53:5).

Therefore, when the thief beside Jesus challenged Him to come down from the cross and save Himself, He could have gotten down from that cross and saved Himself, but then He couldn't have saved you or me. Thus, He remained on the cross, and as the universe looked on, there was no "ram caught in the thicket" to take His place as was the experience of Abraham and Isaac. Had He come down, you would have been that ram; I would have been that ram caught in the thicket. Yes, we would have to die for our transgressions.

No hand of the mighty angel would be raised to stay the hand of the executioner, for He was "the Lamb slain from the foundation of the world" (Rev. 13:8); "who for the joy that was set before Him; endured the cross" (Heb. 12:2). Then they put His body in the tomb, but He rose so we all "may know Him and the power of His resurrection" (Phil. 3:10).

In the volume of the book is revealed the character of the only true God and Jesus Christ whom He sent; the God who is infinite in power; whose love for the human family knows no bounds; who loves us "with an everlasting love" (Jer.31:3); whose "thoughts toward you are thoughts of peace, and not of evil, to give you a future and a hope" (Jer.29:11); the One who made us this wonderful promise: "Let not your heart be troubled; you believed in God, believe also in Me. In My Father's house are many mansions; if it were not so, I would have told you. I go to prepare a place for you. And if I go and prepare a place for you, I will come again and receive you to Myself; that where I am, there you may be also" (John 14:1–3).

Are you ready for Jesus to come? Are you ready to live with Him eternally? Are you becoming more and more like Him? Do you know Him today? Is His prayer being answered in your life, moment by moment, day by day? Are you becoming one with

Him? Are you being sanctified by the truth as it is in Jesus? For these, Jesus prayed (see John 17:3, 17, 21).

"In His prayer to the Father, Christ gave to the world a lesson which should be graven on the mind and soul. 'This is eternal life,' He said, 'that they might know Thee the only true God, and Jesus Christ whom Thou hast sent.' This is true education. It imparts power. The experimental knowledge of God and Jesus Christ, whom He has sent, transforms humanity into the image of God. It gives to humanity the mastery of itself, bringing every impulse and passion of the lower nature under the control of the higher powers of the mind. It makes its possessor a son of God and an heir of heaven. It brings him into communion with the mind of the Infinite, opens to him the rich treasures of the universe." —COL 114.2

"This is the knowledge which is obtained by searching the word of God. And this treasure may be found by every soul who will give all to obtain it." —COL 114.3

Chapter 8

The Experience of the Relationship

"But let him who glories glory in this, that he understands and knows Me" (Jer. 9:24).

The Word tells us that it is by beholding that we become changed. "But we all with open face beholding as in a glass the glory of the Lord, are being changed into the same image from glory to glory, even as by the Spirit of the Lord" (2 Cor. 3:18).

Perhaps no life story in Scripture better demonstrates this principle than the life of Moses. Moses, as he led the children of God from Egyptian bondage and prior, seems to have had extraordinary access to the presence of the God of heaven.

We read in Exodus 3:2–4: "And the angel of the Lord appeared to him in a flame of fire from the midst of a bush. So he looked, and behold, the bush was burning with fire, but the bush was not consumed. Then, Moses said, 'I will now turn aside and see this great sight, why the bush does not burn.' So, when the Lord saw that he turned aside to look, God called to him from the midst of the bush and said, 'Moses, Moses!' and he said, 'here am I.'" As we follow the experience of Moses from this point onward, and his relationship with God, we see a person in constant communication with God, sometimes in the very physical presence of God, far enough not to be consumed by God's presence, yet close enough to be affected by the brightness of God's glory.

In Exodus 34:28–30, we read: "So he was there with the Lord forty days and forty nights…Now it was so, when Moses came down from the Mount Sinai… that Moses did not know that the skin of his face shone while he talked with Him. So, when Aaron and all the children of Israel saw Moses, behold the skin of his face shone and there were afraid to come near him." Though there is a much greater significance attached to the fact that the face of Moses reflected the physical glory of God, it is true that it was the direct result of Moses being in the presence of God for the extended period of time. We could say that Moses spent so much time in the presence of God that he started looking like God. Thus, it is for all of us: the more time we spend with God the better we get to know Him and the more we become like Him.

Moses not only started looking like God but more and more he became like God in character. The more he became like God the more he desired the presence of God, the better he wanted to know God.

We read in Exodus 33:11–18. "So, the Lord spoke to Moses face to face, as a man speaks to his friend..." (Now that is close). "Then Moses said to the Lord, 'see, You say to me, "bring up this people." But You have not let me know whom You will send with me. Yet You have said, "I know you by name, and you have also found grace in My sight." Now therefore, I pray, if I have found grace in Your sight, show me Your way, that I may know You and that I may find grace in Your sight." Moses knew God, but his desire was to know Him more, his longing for the continual presence of God only deepened with time. "Consider that this nation is Your people. And He [God] said, 'My presence will go with you, and I will give you rest.' Then he said to Him, 'if your presence does not go with us, do not bring us up from here. For how then will it be known that Your people and I have found grace in Your sight, except You go with us? So we shall be separate, Your people and I, from all the people who are upon the face of the earth.' So, the Lord said to Moses, 'I will also do this thing that you have spoken; for you have found grace in My sight, and I know you by name.' And he said, 'please show me Your glory.'" Moses seemed to only desire more and more of his God. Oh that we could hunger and thirst for God like he did.

Moses, who had spent so much time in communion with God, so much time in the presence of God, recognized his own powerlessness without God. He knew the importance and power of God's presence in his personal life and for the success of his mission. He knew God and understood that the success of his mission was dependent on God's presence and power. He understood this because he knew that if God was for him, no one could truly be against him. Moreover, he desired a more personal relationship with God. He had been in the presence of God, seemingly closer than any other human being; still he desired to have a deeper experience with God. This epitomizes what it means to "hunger and thirst after righteousness," and the promise was fulfilled in his life. The promise is for all of us; we too may be filled if we would "hunger and thirst after righteousness" (Matt. 5:6).

Moses, having received the assurance of God's presence as he journeyed to the promised land, desired more and more. "Then He said, 'I will make all My goodness pass before you, and I will proclaim the name of the Lord before you. I will be gracious to whom I will be gracious, and I will have compassion on whom I will have compassion.' But He said, 'You cannot see My face; for no man, shall see Me and live.' And the Lord said, 'Here is a place by Me, and you shall stand on the rock. So, it shall be, while My glory passes by, that I will put you in the cleft of the rock, and will cover you with My hand while I passed by. Then I will take away My hand, and you shall see My back but My face shall not be seen'" (Ex. 33:19–23).

God did not disappoint his faithful servant. He allowed Moses to see as much of His physical glory as it was possible for this mortal man to withstand. He showed him the glory of His character: "Now the Lord descended in the cloud and stood with him there, and proclaim the name of the Lord. And the Lord passed before him and proclaimed, the Lord God, merciful and gracious, long-suffering, and abounding in goodness and truth, keeping mercy for thousands, forgiving iniquity and transgression and sin, by no means clearing the guilty" (Ex. 34:5–7). Moses, this once brilliant but rash and impatient prince of Egypt, had now become a faithful servant of God, who over time had gotten to know God as a consequence of his consistent relationship with Him. He had now been changed into the same glory from glory to glory. His character was like that of his Master. It could be said of him: "he had been with Jesus and learned of Him."

Like his Master, he had become the patient, caring leader of his people, and was ready to lay down his life to save them. "And the Lord said to Moses, 'Go, get down! For your people whom you brought out of the land of Egypt have corrupted themselves. They have turned aside quickly out of the way which I commanded them. They have made themselves a molded calf, and worshiped it and sacrificed to it, and said, "This is your god, O Israel, that brought you out of the land of Egypt!"' And the Lord said to Moses, 'I have seen this people and indeed it is a stiff-necked people! Now therefore let me alone, that my wrath may burn hot against them and I may consume them. And I will make of you a great nation.' Then Moses pleaded with the Lord his God, and said: 'Lord, why does Your wrath burn hot against Your people whom You have brought out of the land of Egypt with great power and with a mighty hand'" (Ex. 32:7–11)? "Turn from Your fierce wrath and relent from this harm to Your people," Moses pleaded (v. 12). "So, the Lord relented from the harm which He said He would do to His people" (v. 14). Like His Master, Moses had now become the intercessor for the people he led, and would, like His Master, lay down his life to save them. "Then Moses returned to the Lord and said, 'Oh, these people have committed a great sin, and have made for themselves a god of gold! Yet now, if You will forgive their sin—but if not, I pray, blot me out of Your book which You have written'" (Ex. 32:31, 32). This is how much we can become like our Savior. The more time we spend with Him, the more we get to know Him. Like Moses, we would reflect the character of God; our lives would be a constant manifestation of "love, joy, peace, longsuffering, kindness, goodness, faithfulness, gentleness, self-control" (Gal. 5:22, 23). For we too, "with unveiled face, beholding as in a mirror the glory of the Lord are being transformed into the same image from glory to glory, just as by the spirit of the Lord" (2 Cor. 3:18).

Would you, like so many others have, desire to get to know God through the prayerful study of His Word and allow Him to recreate His image in you? to make you like Him? This is eternal life, Jesus said. There is only one way to become like Him; it is to know Him. This is a most comforting truth: to be like Him is to know Him, to know Him is to be like Him."

Chapter 9

Transformation, Moment by Moment

"Be you holy; for I am holy" (1 Pet. 1:16).

"Grace and peace be multiplied unto you through the knowledge of God, and of Jesus our Lord, according as His divine power hath given unto us all things that pertain unto life and godliness, through the knowledge of Him that hath called us to glory and virtue: whereby are given unto us exceeding great and precious promises: that by these ye might be partakers of the divine nature, having escaped the corruption that is in the world through lust" (2 Pet. 1:2–4).

"Before the believer is held out the wonderful possibility of being like Christ, obedient to all the prin-

ciples of the law. But of himself man is utterly unable to reach this condition. The holiness that God's word declares he must have before he can be saved is the result of the working of divine grace as he bows in submission to the discipline and restraining influences of the Spirit of truth. Man's obedience can be made perfect only by the incense of Christ's righteousness, which fills with divine fragrance every act of obedience. The part of the Christian is to persevere in overcoming every fault. Constantly he is to pray to the Savior to heal the disorders of his sin-sick soul. He has not the wisdom or the strength to overcome; these belong to the Lord, and He bestows them on those who in humiliation and contrition seek Him for help." —AA 532.1

"The work of transformation from unholiness to holiness is a continuous one. Day by day God labors for man's sanctification, and man is to co-operate with Him, putting forth persevering efforts in the cultivation of right habits. He is to add grace to grace; and as he thus works on the plan of addition, God works for him on the plan of multiplication. Our Savior is always ready to hear and answer the prayer of the contrite heart, and grace and peace are multiplied to His faithful ones. Gladly He grants them the blessings they need in their struggle against the evils that beset them." —AA 532.2

Chapter 10

An Awesome Privilege

"That you would walk worthy of God who calls you into His own Kingdom and glory" (1. Thess. 2:12).

The awesome privilege is ours to be like our Savior as we get to know Him. Isn't that a most amazing thing? With this awesome privilege comes a great responsibility, one which determines our eternal destiny. To know Him is our passport to the kingdom; to live with Him eternally, we must become like Him. The only way to become like Him is to get to know Him as He is revealed in His Word; there is simply no other way. Yes, the bar may be seen as too high, but the bar has not moved in about 6,000 years. It has been the same for every generation. The standard has been the same place for Adam, Enoch, Noah, Abraham, Isaac, Jacob, Moses, Elijah, Daniel, and his Hebrew friends; the same for Peter, James, John, and the countless millions who will have eternal life with Jesus. They all got to know Him by the experience of a relationship and in the process, became like Him. Perhaps we could say that Enoch, Moses, and Elijah have already use their passports to the kingdom; already stamped "ENTERED" because they have already entered. The others await the second coming of our Savior, when the promise of 1 John 3:2 will be realized: "Dear friends, now we are children of God, and what we will be has not yet been made known. **But we know that when Christ appears, we shall be like Him, for we shall see Him as He is" (NIV).**

The good news is that you are not alone in this grand endeavor. Those who have become like God were not super human. In fact they were very much like us. "Elijah was a human being, even as we are" (James 5:17, NIV). God would never ask the impossible of us. When He asks us to be holy because He is holy (see1 Pet. 1:16), it is not to set us up for failure, but because He knows we can be holy. He knows that by His power we can be sanctified by getting to know Him through His Word. Jesus puts it this way in John 17:17: "Sanctify them by Your truth, Your word is truth." He has not forgotten who we are: "For as the heavens are high above the earth, so great is His mercy toward those who fear Him; As far as the east is from the west, so far has He removed our transgressions from us. As a father pities his children, so the Lord pities those who fear Him. **For He knows our frame; and remembers that we are dust"**

(Ps. 103:11–14). He knows that we are powerless to achieve the transformation of character that makes us like Him. He knows that we can no more change ourselves than can a leopard change its spots (see Jer. 13:23). So, it was with those in every generation who had become like Him. We have the assurance that we can do all things through Christ who strengthens us (Phil. 4:13).

Chapter 11

Your Forever Companion, the Holy Spirit

"But grow in the grace and knowledge of our Lord and Savior Jesus Christ" (2 Pet. 3:18).

"Beholding Christ means studying His life as given in His Word. We are to dig for truth as for hidden treasure. We are to fix our eyes upon Christ. When we take Him as our personal Savior, this gives us boldness to approach the throne of grace. By beholding, we become changed—morally assimilated to the One who is perfect in character. By receiving His imputed righteousness, through the transforming power of the Holy Spirit, we become like Him…" —12MR 55.3

We will get to know God as we engage in a prayerful, diligent study of His Word, where His character of love is so adequately revealed. As we look at the process of becoming like Him as a consequence of getting to know Him, we are mindful of this fact: we cannot reveal Him to ourselves; neither can our pastor, priest, or any religious leader. As we turn the pages of the Scriptures, only God can reveal Himself to us. "For what man knows the things of a man except the spirit of the man which is in him? Even so no one knows the things of God except the Spirit of God" (1 Cor. 2:11). The Holy Spirit reveals God to us as we study His Word. Nehemiah puts it this way: "You also gave Your good Spirit to instruct them" (Neh. 9:20). Jesus puts it this way: "However, when He, the Spirit of truth has come, He will guide you into all truth" (John 16:13). "But when the helper comes, whom I shall send to you from the Father, the Spirit of truth who proceeds from the Father, He will testify of Me" (John 15:26). Yes, the bar is high, but God has promised us the power of His Holy Spirit to lead us in the understanding of who He is, His character, and as we behold God thus revealed, we are transformed into His likeness by that same Spirit. What an amazing experience! "But we all, with unveiled face, beholding as in a mirror the glory of the Lord, are being transformed into the same image from glory to glory, just as by the Spirit of the Lord" (2 Cor. 3:18). What an awesome privilege is ours! We can become like our wonderful Savior as we get to know Him, as He is revealed in His Word by the Holy Spirit.

Do you Know Him today? Are you being sanctified by the truth as it is in Jesus? Are you becoming one with Him as He is one with the Father? Are you becoming more and more like God as a result of a consistent relationship with Him? This was the burden of His soul as He prayed to His Father for you and me. The Father longs to answer the prayer of Jesus in the life of each of us. Our eternal destiny is dependent on it.

Chapter 12
Stay Connected to the Source of Power

"Not by might, nor by power, but by My Spirit"
(Zech. 4:6).

Jesus said, "Abide in Me and I in you. As the branch, cannot bear fruit of itself, unless it abides in the vine, neither can you, unless you abide in Me. I am the vine, you are the branches: He that abideth in Me, and I in him, the same bringeth forth much fruit: for without Me ye can do nothing" (John 15:4–5, KJV).

The grapevine was a very well-known vine to the Jewish people. From the very earliest times, vines and vineyards have been mentioned in Scripture. Therefore, when Jesus spoke of Himself as the vine, the language was understood by all who heard. Think of the grapevine with its branches. As long as the branches were connected to the vine, they had life. When the branch is severed from the vine, it dies because it could no longer receive from the vine what it needed to maintain life. So, it is with us: as we stay connected to Jesus, we receive of His life which enables us to be like Him. Our lives then are fruitful like His and God is glorified. "By this is My Father glorified, that you bear much fruit; so you will be My disciples" (John 15:8).

The branch being connected to the vine demonstrates the closeness of the relationship we must have with our Savior. As the branch draws the life-sustaining nutrients from the vine moment by moment, day by day, so we receive from the life of Jesus as we maintain a close and consistent relationship with Him. Jesus died that we may again become the sons and daughters of God; that we may become like Him. Becoming like our Savior as a consequence of a close and consistent relationship with Him is a most wonderful privilege. A close and consistent relationship with Him is not optional; it is an obligation, if we are to live with the redeemed.

Jesus demonstrated by His life of dependence on the Father what we can be if we abide in Him. He assures us that we can live a life above sin like He did. "I have kept My Father's commandments", Jesus said; and John writes, "he who says he abides in Him ought himself also to walk just as He walked" (John 15:10; 1 John 2:6). Then we can bear much fruit to the glory of God, because we have the same mind as Jesus.

"Therefore, if there is any consolation in Christ, if any comfort of love, if any fellowship of the Spirit, if any affection and mercy, fulfill my joy being of one accord, of one mind....Let this mind be in you which was also in Christ Jesus" (Phil. 2:1–2, 5).

God has made every provision for us to become like Him. If we would receive the most from this awesome privilege, our relationship with Him will be as close and consistent as the relationship of the vine and its branches.

How well do you know Him today? How much time do you spend in prayerful study of His life as revealed in His Word?

Do you know Him today? Are you becoming like Him? It doesn't matter where you have been, where you are in the process of getting to know Him, whether you are meeting Him for the first time or for yet another time. The good news is that you can leave the past behind, whatever that past may have been. Lay hold on God's promised power and like the Apostle Paul, "forgetting those things which are behind and reaching forward to those things which are ahead, I press toward the goal for the prize of the upward call of God in Christ Jesus" (Phil. 3:13–14).

This "high calling of God in Christ Jesus;" this call to holiness, to righteousness as it is in Jesus is within the reach of every person who earnestly seeks "for the excellency of the knowledge of Christ Jesus my Lord..." "That [they] may know Him, and the power of His resurrection." Yes, my friends, you can know Him, and by His grace you can be like Him. "Not by might (your strength) nor by power, but by My Spirit," says the Lord of hosts" (Zech. 4:6). The assurance is ours, that we can be all God wants us to be, that we can live in conformity to His will. "For this is the will of God, even your sanctification" (1 Thess. 4:3).

Yes, friends, the will of God is that we be sanctified and made holy as He is Holy; that we be righteous as He is righteous; that we be like Him as we prepare to live with Him eternally; that we become one with Jesus as He is one with the Father; that we know Him. This was the desire of the heart of Jesus as He made a most impassioned plea to the Father for His disciples and those who should believe in Him through their word. "I do not pray for these alone, but also for those who will believe in Me through their word; that they all may be one, as You, Father, are in Me and I in You; that they also may be one in Us" (John 17:20–21). "Sanctify them by Your truth, Your word is truth" (John 17:17) "And this is eternal life, that they may know You, the only true God, and Jesus Christ whom you have sent" (John 17:3). **To know Him is to be like Him. To be like Him is to know Him. This is a most comforting truth: A truth so central to our salvation, that it shouldn't surprise us that Jesus prayed for it three times in the same prayer. Yes, friends, Jesus prayed for you to know Him, for your sanctification, and for your oneness with Him and the Father.**

The only questions that remain are: has the prayer of Jesus our Savior been answered in your life? in our lives? Are we becoming more and more like Him as a consequence of a consistent relationship with Him?

May "the peace of God, which surpasses all understanding…guard your hearts and minds through

Christ Jesus" and "may the God of peace Himself sanctify you completely; and may your whole spirit, soul, and body be preserved blameless at the coming of our Lord Jesus Christ" (Phil. 4:7; 1 Thess. 5:23).